Positive

Negative World

Change Your Life – Positive Self Talk – Positive Thoughts!

By Dylan j Cameron

Table of Contents

Introduction

I want to thank you and congratulate you for downloading the book, Positive Thinking in a Negative World.

These days, it's so easy to berate yourself for almost everything. When something goes wrong, you might say it's because you don't deserve the good things in life, or that you are being persecuted. This way of thinking only derails you from living the good life that you actually deserve.

And yet, oftentimes, you allow yourself to get lost in this way of thinking—when in fact, you could do the opposite. And what is the opposite, then? Well, it's all about thinking positively, of course!

This book contains proven steps and strategies on how to get yourself to think positively—and how you could appreciate yourself and express gratitude for your life, among others

After reading this book, you'd have a renewed appreciation for yourself—and you'd help yourself realize that you can do it all, and that life is actually good—all by making use of positive thoughts.

Read this book now, and get on your way to being a happier you.

Thanks again for downloading this book, I hope you enjoy it!

If you are on a self-improvement journey I would highly recommend the books-

Building Self-Esteem and Confidence; A Practical guide for self-improvement

Communication Skills Master Class; Get comfortable Talking to Anyone

Both Amazing books are by Lisa j Roberts

Here's the thing: It is so common for people to embrace the bad things in life. It's like, people find it easier to understand that negative things can happen instead of thinking that positive things CAN and WILL actually happen.

Ask yourself this: how does negative thinking help you, actually? Does it make your life better? Or does it just blind you into thinking that life will always be the way it is now—and that it cannot get better?

It's not hard to understand how people have gotten that way. After all, there are certain things that happen in life that could break you and make you hard. There are things in life that could really shatter those rose-coloured lenses of yours.

But you know what? Maybe, it's high time that you awaken your inner child again—and start believing in positive things once more.

Start Small

Of course, it's not that easy to do—especially when you have been through so much in life, but you can start simply by thinking about these things:

1. Acknowledge the good things in life—and in you, as a person. When all the negative thoughts seem to blind you, remember that there are a lot of amazing things in your life—and you know what? That's a good start to remind you that you can be thankful for your life—and that other great, beautiful things can happen, too!

2.   Find something good in each day. Another easy way of helping yourself embrace the positive things in life is by trying to find something good in each day. These things don't have to be big. For example, maybe your favourite artist has released a new album, you got to talk to an old friend, or maybe, the weather was seriously good. It's easy to think positive when you actually focus on the positive things in life—just like what have been mentioned here!

3.   Be happy about the good things in you and in your life. Bask in them. Realize that there is nothing wrong with appreciating the good things that you have—because if you don't, you'd surely feel hollow when the negative things arise.

4.   Find the silver lining in every dark cloud. Yes, it is absolutely hard to do—but should that stop you from trying to do so? Of course not. So, maybe you broke up with your partner—take your time to cry, but also remember that now, you have all the chances in the world to find yourself again, and get back on the fun, dating scene! Maybe, you've lost something—well, maybe, it's just a way of making space for something better. Before you get down and depressed, just try to realize that bad days may come—but that does not mean the good days won't anymore. A life without any challenge is not really a life worth living.

5.   See the possibilities in life. No matter who you are, and no matter what your life's been like, you always have a chance to change yourself for the better—and to experience the best things in life. Do not deprive yourself of this thought.

6.   Continue walking in the path of your life with positive perspective. In life, there will always be hurdles—but those hurdles should not stop you from walking towards your goals. Don't let your dreams die just because you have experienced hardships before. What separates great people from mediocre ones is their zest for life—the way they stand up after each fall. Concentrate on what you can still become, instead of on what you have been.

See? By simply embracing the thought of positive thinking, a lot of good things can already happen in your life. Just think about all the great things that could happen next.

Chapter 2 Stress and Anxiety

It seems lot of people find it difficult to remember that stress and anxiety is a very real problem in life, that affects many people all over the world. It affects us on different levels, physically as well as mentally and emotionally. If we come under an overwhelming amount of stress and anxiety, this can and will create a lot of tension in the body. Stress can physically poison the bloodstream and cause a lot of health problems that can often be misdiagnosed and ultimately treated the wrong way.

A distinct disadvantage comes with the mistreatment of dangerous problems with chemical drugs that ultimately cause more side effects and issues to pile onto the original cause of the disorder. The underlying cause continues to go untreated, and your symptoms can just become exacerbated by the medication or further exposure to the cause of your stress and anxiety.

This can be dangerous for more than one reason. People who have high bouts of stress and anxiety are often looking for a cure. Many times, they look in the wrong place for that and wind up in a terrible cycle of narcotics abuse or other forms of self-medication that do not work and actually harm you. Some people begin to withdraw and become more afraid of social interactions. Sometimes you may find yourself distracting yourself with television and movies or other forms of media so that you do not have to deal with your feelings on a day-to-day basis, because they are unpleasant and difficult to understand. Going through stress can be extremely dangerous for us, both physically and mentally, and if we are high strung, this pollution of the body can make us more vulnerable to diseases and prevent new cells from forming that can help us to fight off harmful invaders in the body.

Stress can physically affect us in many ways. We can have frequent headaches, a hard time with swallowing or with keeping our mouth wet. It can cause us to feel dizzy and bring our heart rates very high. It can cause a lot of problems in our relationships because many times we feel very irritable and nervous. Sometimes we have breathing problems or we tend to sweat and twitch a lot more than is typically considered normal. Sometimes we are full of aches and pains that we don't know how we got. Other times, it can make it difficult for us to learn things or focus on schoolwork or other important tasks in our daily lives because it seriously affects our ability to concentrate.

There is too much energy in the blood that is not released physically and it can cause hormones to be released into the body that can begin to seriously harm us in a physical way.

This is particularly dangerous because it can suppress our immune system and lead to a whole slew of different diseases. If our immune system is not functioning well enough, that leaves us vulnerable to just about any bacteria that we come into contact with, even if on a normal day we would be feeling great and unaffected by those germs. It can cause many digestive disorders, including uncomfortable bouts of gastrointestinal problems.

This is because stress and anxiety are closely tied to our physical bodies, and when we feel nervous, we tend to feel nauseated or strange in the stomach. This is a physical response to stress and it can lead to even more difficulties in your digestive system;

Stress and anxiety has even been connected to a lot of dangerous issues with our muscles and our hearts. Many people who suffer from stress and hypertension for a long time tend to develop diseases in their hearts and suffer from heart attacks. This can be lethal and can cause extremely uncomfortable physical pain. Muscle tension is nothing to scoff at either, and this physical results of stress and anxiety is also dangerous and uncomfortable. It's another thing that can lead to headaches and other physiological issues.

Many people who have suffered from extreme bouts of stress and anxiety may find themselves dealing with intense bouts of short-term memory loss. While they may be able to understand and remember things that have happened in the past or over a course of time, extreme memory loss is common among many people who have suffered from traumatic and highly stressful events. Even if you have not suffered from trauma necessarily, if you are somebody who has a highly prone disposition to stress and anxiety, you may find yourself forgetting things short-term, such as where you put your glasses or if you bought coffee or not.

This type of memory loss can be extremely disruptive to your everyday routine, so if you can find a way to cope with it, that is the best thing that you can do for yourself and your body at any given time. Many people have a hard time coping with stress and anxiety, because the way that the modern world is structured is not particularly encourage us to thrive and relax. If we are stressed out and panicking over little things, it may actually be because we have some kind of a stress or anxiety disorder that causes us a lot of difficulty in functioning in our day-to-day lives. A lot of people have a difficult time focusing their attention on pursuits that may leave them feeling more fulfilled and rewarded after a hard day of work.

People work hard so that they can continue to survive in today's society, but it does not leave a whole lot of time for you to get the things done that you feel will bring you the most joy and satisfaction. This can leave us feeling afraid for our own security if we decide to try and pursue more endeavours toward the things that we enjoy the most, and it can cause difficulties in our close and interpersonal relationships with other people because we are not able to fully immerse ourselves in the things that matter to us. This can make us extremely unhappy and irritable, causing a lot of negative tensions to arise between close family members and friends.

When something is hard to understand and to deal with is when we become consumed by stress and anxiety. When this happens, our brains are physically affected and it can sometimes cause us to act out irrationally and make connections that should not be made. For example, we may believe that something is our fault because we were simply there, we are a failure in life for making one mistake, or we may think that if we do not do something right on time, it will be the end of the world.

These habits and negative ways of thinking can actually be very dangerous and disrupt our inner peace. Fortunately, there is a solution that many people have overlooked over the years, but it has started to get the attention that it deserves. The solution is positive thinking.

Chapter 3 Learn to Appreciate Yourself

Next, it's also time that you learn how to appreciate yourself.

See, the problem with most people is that they focus on caring for and appreciating others too much that they forget to love and appreciate the most important person in their lives: themselves.

When you don't appreciate yourself as much as you should, you begin to fall into the traps of pain and depression. You tend to settle for less than what you deserve. You don't begin to give yourself the praises and the compliments that you need to hear, and instead, you allow the demons in your head to eat you up—and eat you whole.

It's time to stop these things. Follow the tips below, and you'd learn how to appreciate yourself more!

1. Make way for self-approval. The thing about life is that not everyone will appreciate you, and it's true. You can try your best—but certain people would not. And you know what? There's nothing you can do about that. But what you can do is just learn how to give yourself some self-approval. Tell yourself that you're great and amazing the way you are. Tell yourself that you can do great things. When you become your number 1 fan, you won't be so keen on getting the approval of others. You won't be so sad when they don't give you their approval—because it won't really matter. When you detach your mind from being so obsessed with what others have to say, you'd feel like a big weight will be off your shoulders, for sure!

2. Be grateful for who you are! Not everyone gets the chance to live, and you have. Thank yourself for actually living through each day—even the bad days. Be your own inspiration. Each day, try to

write what you're thankful for in your life. Try to be happy with how your mind and body are. Be thankful that you had the chance to live your life again.

3. Appreciate what you have deeply. Sure, you may say you're thankful for something—but do you really believe what you're saying? You won't be extremely appreciative of yourself and of what you have without thinking about what you're actually thankful for. For example, maybe you're thankful for the fact that you have a house to live in—that you have such a comfortable bed, and that your couch is plus. Maybe, you're thankful that you have been promoted at work. Maybe, you're thankful for your pets. Maybe, you're thankful for this and that—there are so many things you can be thankful for, and when you become specific about them, it's actually easy to understand why your life is actually good—and not the other way around! Learn how to be content with what you have, instead of wishing that you can get this and that without being appreciative of what you have.

4. Learn to go easy on yourself. The world is full of critics. People will always tell you that you're not good, you need to do more, be more, etc. Sometimes, people would also be harsh—and when you're a negative thinker, you'd probably just end up believing them. Again: there are critics who want you to do better, but there are also others who are just hell bent on destroying you. What you can do now is make sure that you learn how to prevent yourself from jumping on that critical bandwagon. Don't bash yourself. Lift yourself up and say that you can do better, but don't put too much pressure on yourself that you end up not being able to enjoy life anymore. Do what you have to do—and whether or not people will appreciate it? Well, that is up to them.

5. Try to do something nice for yourself each day. There is nothing wrong with having "me" time each day. Contrary to popular belief, this does not have to be expensive. Rather, you can do anything that makes you happy: be it eating at your favourite restaurant,

buying yourself a pack of your favourite fries, putting on makeup, or even looking at Instagram. When you do something good for yourself, you get to remind yourself that even if you'd have a long day at work tomorrow, there are still things that you can look forward to. Putting these things away could damage you—and that's not what you'd want to happen.

6. Lighten your responses. There are things in life that could really make you mad, but by dwelling on them, you'd just harden your heart and think about negative things—when you can actually focus on the positive. When something makes you mad, take a deep breath, and think before engaging in confrontation. Think if it's actually worth it—or if you can just let it go. And more often than not, just allow yourself to let it go—and watch yourself breathe.

7. Just choose to be brave. Remind yourself that life really won't always be easy—but what you can do is choose to remain brave through it all. You don't have to pick fights to be brave. The fact that you're allowing yourself to stay strong even though life could be such a mess? That's one of the best kinds of bravery there is.

8. Think Empowering thoughts! Don't be afraid to dream big! Don't be afraid to wish for the great things in life. Work for them—and stay positive, and chances are, you'd actually have the chance to have them in your life!

9. And, learn to love yourself unconditionally. Other people won't always love you whole. They won't love you for who you are and who you're not. And you know what? You don't have to be one of them. Promise to love yourself unconditionally—because when you become your own best friend, life definitely becomes easier!

By learning to appreciate yourself, you begin to get on the road to healing—and you open yourself up to better opportunities in life.

Chapter 4 Exercises For Positivity

Once we have recognized our tendency to think negatively we can start taking some very important simple steps toward changing that thinking. First we need to accept that we do need to change our current thought patterns and that we are more than able to do so. We have already seen that positive thoughts are supportive to our wellbeing. The science has demonstrated this greatly in many areas from health to longevity but we don't really need science to show us that. I believe that most people are aware how our negative thoughts are not allowing us to be and function at our best. We have also witnessed through experience in our own lives how much more attractive and fun it is to be around truly positive people than those who are constantly in a negative state.

BELIEVE THAT YOU CAN CHANGE

Believing that you can intentionally change the way you think is sometimes more of an obstacle for the negative thinkers to overcome. They may recognize that it can be done but somehow they have conditioned themselves to believe that positive change is something beyond their own abilities; a gift that others have but which they have not been provided with. If you are one of those people I urge you not to give up. Instead focus on the fact that you want to change your mindset and tackle some of the exercises below on a daily basis for just one month. I am convinced if you do that you will begin to see results.

START FROM THE BEGINNING

Always try to start your day on a positive foot. Before even getting out of bed, as you lay in a state of only semi wakefulness, try to think of three things that you could be grateful for. It can be any three things and even if they appear selfish indulgences don't let that put you off. Focus on each one of those three things. Play with them around in your mind until you really get a sense of them. Don't use the same three things every day or the process will lose meaning and become mere ritual. Depending on how firm a hold negative thinking has on you it may be difficult at first but within a week the exercise will have become easier because you mind will begin to start looking out for small things to be grateful for throughout the course of each day.

BE AWARE OF NEGATIVITY

As you get up and begin you daily routine train you mind to look out for negative thoughts. As soon as you spot one replace it with a counter thought that is positive. Many negative thoughts are re-occurring. The same thought will continue to thrust itself into your thinking throughout the course of the day. Even this can be looked at from a positive point of view because each time the negative thought begins you are countering it with a differing positive thought so that you can be sure that you have really understood the problem and have considered all the positive angles against it.

STOP CATASTROPHIZING

Instead of catastrophizing and imagining the worst case scenario for any upcoming situation turn that thinking on its head and think of the most positive outcome and how you would deal with that.

FILTERING AND POLARIZING

These are two common traits that are employed by negative thinkers that we must avoid. Filtering involves mentally exaggerating the negative and minimizing the positive whilst polarizing involves thinking of things as being either totally positive or totally negative with nothing in between. We all do a bit of both from time to time but as we get better at positive thinking and as we are now aware of the traits we can overcome these thought processes by employing the methods we are now working our way through.

USE BREATHING

At any stage that you feel stress then look for the negative thought that almost definitely lies behind it. Counter that thought and focus on slow deep breathing while you do so. In any stress situation our breathing becomes shallow and rapid in preparation for the fight or flight response that we have inherited from nature. Slow, deliberate and controlled breathing helps alleviate this and sends more oxygen to the brain allowing for more reasoned thinking processes to take place.

FEED THE MIND

Feed you mind with messages of self-assertion and confidence. Focus on being the person you want to be and kill any negative thoughts that pop up telling you that you cannot be that person. Make mental statements such as "I am a good salesperson." or "I am a loving and capable parent." Statements of this nature may seem pointless but they are feeding you mind with positive thoughts and filling space that may otherwise have been filled with negative thoughts. Many people find it beneficial to write down positive statements during the course of the day. The physical act of writing that we are able to do almost without thinking helps prolong a positive thought that we may have considered less were it merely run through our thought processes.

STATE THE POSITIVE

Remember to not only have positive thoughts but to make positive statements during conversation. You need to start projecting a more positive personality. Merely thinking positively is not enough. If you are to gain the full benefit of a positive mindset, then you need to be seen by others to be a positive person as you interact in your daily life. This will have two benefits. It will make you focus on the positive when you express yourself and it will start to induce a positive atmosphere amongst those around you which in turn means you benefit by being part of a positive environment.

TEACH AND HELP OTHERS

Another great way to engender positivity in yourself is to teach it to others. Some of these techniques you are starting out with would be really beneficial to your kids if they were to adopt them early in their lives before their minds cling too firmly to negative thoughts. Think of how much easier their lives will be if they start out as positive thinkers filled with a positive self-image from an early age. Once you become known as being a positive person people will begin to ask you how you manage to always see things differently to the crowd and you will be able to drop in some of the techniques you are learning here. Teaching it will not only raise your status but will further drive the positive images you wish to inculcate into your character.

LOOK TO BE GRATEFUL

Gratitude and positivity are two sides of the same coin. It is almost impossible to be grateful about something without being positive about it. You have started your day off on a grateful note. Now look for small things to continually being

grateful about as you go through your day. As your mind adapts to this new way of thinking, being grateful for things will become almost second nature. Suddenly your eyes will open to a whole new world that was always there but which your senses had become dulled to. Appreciating them and dwelling on them just a little is one of the most positive things you will ever learn to do.

GREAT PHYSICAL BENEFITS

We have seen how our minds can have positive effects on our bodies in terms of health. Because the mind and body are so closely interlinked there are things that we can do physically that influence our mental attitude. Getting out of bed half an hour earlier each day can have a dramatic effect on your mental state and the amount you can get done. Of course some people are not morning people and the mere whisper of them having to get up any earlier can send a shiver down their spines. I believe that the physical aspect of getting out of bed is linked to out mental approach to it and that is why I have waited toward the end of the book before bringing up the subject.

As your thinking becomes more positive you will find that you look at things so differently compared to the way you used to. You will begin to see the positive aspects even in such things as getting up earlier. The same can be said for exercise and eating correctly. As you focus on the positive, that link between body and mind will become more apparent and you will begin to naturally lean toward making more positive decisions about how you treat your body.

I am not here to advocate a total change in your life but you should be aware, and look forward to the fact, that resetting the mind will eventually see changes across whole swathes of your lifestyle. Like me, you may begin to even change the material you feed your mind with. I tend to be put off by books and television programs that I now perceive as portraying negative themes.

It was never my intention to change in those areas; it has simply become a spinoff of a more positive mindset. The changes I have made to my diet and health regimes have required no great effort either. They are simply sensible adaptations that came about naturally as a result of thinking of the positive benefits those changes would have.

"Positive thinking is more than just a tagline. It changes the way we behave. And I firmly believe that when I am positive, it not only makes me better, but it also makes those around me better." Harvey Mackay.

Chapter 5 Try to See the Positive in Every Situation

Life is not perfect and it won't always be a bed of roses. But when faced with gruelling situations, you just have to remind yourself to look the other way. While it may be hard, it's actually doable. Here's what you can do:

1. **Prevent yourself from making the situation worse in your head.** You may have the tendency to overplay things in your head, especially when something negative happens in your life. It is not uncommon for humans to obsess over things—especially when they feel like something else could've been done, or that maybe, they have not done enough to prevent the situation. If you see yourself doing this, remind yourself that things have already happened. There is no use crying over spilt milk and there's no way for you to go back to a certain moment to "change things". However, you can remind yourself to focus on what you can still do now—and what you can do in the future to make sure that those things won't happen again, or that if they do, at least, you'd be ready for them. Don't let yourself feel worse by feeding yourself negative thoughts.

2. **Have an inventory of positive memories.** Let's say someone you love leaves your life. In any way, it's definitely hard. It will hurt, and at times, you might wish that things should be different, but when you look back on what's good in your life, it anchors you down. It makes you realize that although things are certainly not perfect now, there would always be good days. So for example, you lost someone. Maybe, it'll help if you could focus on the great memories you share—instead of the part that this someone is gone. Because although it hurts, would you rather choose that you did not have this person—or even a pet—in your life at all? Probably not, right? So, just focus on the positive—and think that there is a reason why this happened.

3. Try to understand why you're angry—and then see how you can let the anger out. Scream, write, talk to the person you're angry at, etc. But afterwards, let it go. Don't dwell on it. Once you have aired your side out—that's that. Don't try to pick the situation apart or obsesses over it as it'll just take over your life—and not in a positive manner. You don't want to let anger or an obsession about something take over your whole life because it would just make things worse for you—these things will just make you feel like you don't have a life worth living, and that is not true at all. Your life is worth living—maybe you should just start trying to appreciate it.

4. Revaluate your rules in life. Are people really making you angry? Or, maybe, it's you who's making yourself angry because you have unrealistic expectations? Learn to understand that your life is different from everybody else's—so do not try to put up the same rules as others.

5. Rules do not have to be applied in every circumstance. Remember that each event that happens in your life is different from the rest, so do not be someone who feels the need to make use of the same rules for different situations in life. That just won't work.

6. Do not deny your anger—but don't let it control you, either. Recognize why you're angry, but don't let it rule over your life.

7. Try to find the lesson in every situation. Certain things happen in life because they have to. There are lessons you have to learn in life that you won't learn anywhere else. Challenges are hard and that's for sure, and more often than not, when these negative things happen, you do not really understand them. But when you have calmed down a bit, maybe you could remind yourself that although you do not understand why right now, there are reasons why things happen. Problems happen so you could be shaped into the person

you're supposed to be, and so you can let go of being so focused on the menial things in life. When you realize that life happens the way it should, you learn how to see the positive in every situation—and that could really help you breeze through life better!

8. Control the way you respond to things. Have you ever heard of the saying that life is just 10% of what happens to you, and 99% of how you react to it?

Sure, life may not always be easy, and there are days when you'd feel like it's just one full bed of challenges. But, the thing is, you actually don't have to let those challenges rule your life—it's how you react to them, and how you turn your life after them, that matters. You become free when you get to pause between the stimulus and the response; when you decide how to react to something before reacting right away.

9. Let go. Once you have aired your frustrations, and once you know you have done something to recognize it, learn to let go. You don't have to let this anger make decisions for you every day of your life. When you let go, you begin to give yourself the chance to live life freely—and not by being attached to things that you probably should forget about already.

By trying to see what's good in every situation, you begin to live life in a lighter manner—which could bring forth a lot of great things for you!

Chapter 6 Positive Affirmations and Positive Energy

Using positive affirmations and developing positive energy in life are both important. Affirmations can make you see what's good in life. They make you realize that life can be good—and will be good—but only if you believe in it enough.

Positive Affirmations

First, sit down on the grass or on a mat and visualize your happy place. It can be a place that makes you feel serene—or your so-called sanctuary, or a place you would like to visit in the future. Focus on that and on nothing else. It's also a form of visualization.

Then, repeat these affirmations:

My own reality could be created from what I want the universe to reflect through me.

I pray for the kindness and benevolence of the Divine Power to envelop me; to help me love myself the way I deserve to be loved.

My life is a mystery of divinity and beauty; I will praise and love it at all times.

I will not be carried away by what my mind dictates; I'll learn how to listen to my mind.

I trust myself, and make choices that are healthy for me.

I trust in the goodness of life; I trust that the choices I make will help me grow and transform.

I can resolve my life's challenges through strong will.

Just like a star or a tree, I feel safe and secure.

I'd breathe, and not be in a rush at all times; I'd learn to appreciate life for what it really is.

I stand for justice, and truth; I stand for my values.

I pray for those who are neutral—so they could finally see where they belong, and whom they should be friends or enemies with.

I pray for the entire universe to be at peace; for life to be great on earth.

I pray for everyone on earth to have peace in their hearts, and learn how to live their best lives.

I pray for difficult people—so they could also see the light, and be good to others so life could be better for everyone.

I have a right to speak my truth.

I pray for love and kindness to grow in the hearts of my friends; for love and kindness to rule their lives, and make them happy in this world.

I love my life, and I trust myself.

I live an authentic life.

I have integrity.

I have a right to be here on earth; my presence certainly means something.

I can stand on my own two feet; I am grounded and stable.

I can reach the highest peak of my life by means of being happy and at peace.

I am unfolding; by observing myself, I could be my own person; my real person.

I can express myself through art, writing, and speech.

I can communicate my feelings with ease.

I can be at peace because I meditate; I won't let the world hurt me.

I am protected. I am peaceful, and secure.

I am honest in my communication; I am open, and I am clear.

I am grateful for the challenges in my life; I have the capacity to overcome them.

I am connected to my body; I am deeply rooted.

I am a peaceful, I am serene.

Cultivate Positive Energy

Then, make sure that you'd cultivate positive energy by doing the following:

1. Always tell yourself that no matter what situation you're in, you can figure things out, and you can move on from there. There's no reason for you to get stuck, because at the end of the day, there's always tomorrow, and there's always a way out. There is always a solution.

2. Smile! Hey, it's true. It does take more muscles to frown than to smile. So, instead of wasting all that energy to cultivate negativity, just go ahead and smile. You never know who needs to see that smile, and who knows? Maybe, someone's day could be better because you smiled at him. Plus, smiling also helps you realize that the day could be beautiful and that there's nothing wrong with being happy and that's why you should never let a day pass without smiling!

3. Know that you can be frustrated, but you don't have to let those frustrations rule your life. As they say, there is nothing permanent in the world. Even problems and bad situations come and go so it would be useless to grieve over a temporary situation. Sure, you can be sad, but never ever think that this is all there is in life.

4. Don't fall into a pattern. Routine is good when it helps you grow and when it helps you become a better person, but when you find

yourself in situations that just keep on repeating themselves and makes you feel bad about yourself, maybe it's high time that you change something. Don't be scared of change because sometimes, it is exactly what you need in life.

5.   Share your stories, and listen to what others have to say, too. The world is so much bigger than just the four corners of your room, or heck, your office cubicle. Research has it that communication is capable of making people feel better because it's great to be able to open up your heart and mind, and it's great to be able to listen to what people have to say because you can learn so much from them.

6.   Find work that matters for YOU. Sure, there may be so many jobs out there that could give you all the financial benefits that you need, and may make others see you in such a way that you can be considered "successful", or "rich", or "enviable", but ask yourself: Are you happy with this job? Does this job make you feel like you're able to use your talents and skills? Or does it make you feel dumb and down? At the end of the day, you're not going to work for all these people—you are going to work for you, so choose a job that challenges you, and makes you happy, and you'll feel like you're not even working at all. And remember, if you choose a job that you like, even if there may be some downtimes, and even if there may be times when you'd feel like you're down, if you like your job, you'd find it easy to get back on track.

7.   Forgive. Don't hold grudges. Sure, there are some things that can really make anyone angry, but at the end of the day, if you hold on to anger, you're just damaging yourself more than you damage the people you're angry at. More so, if you're the type of person who doesn't know how to forgive himself, it will be so hard for you to move on and see that life is so much more than what you think you know. Forgiveness is tantamount to being happy.

8.   Never forget what you have achieved. You know what? It's not wrong to actually look back on the past, and recognize your successes. It's always good to realize that you are good at something, instead of just focusing on your weaknesses. It won't be arrogant to remind yourself that you are capable of a lot of things because of what you have achieved in the past. This way, you'd also want to learn more and be more because you know that you can do better, and that you have a lot of things to be thankful for.

9.   Don't cultivate envy and jealousy. Wouldn't it be better to live in a world where people try to help each other out instead of pull each other down? Sure, you may not be as rich or as pretty or as tall as someone else, but you also have all these things that they don't have. You have skills and talents that people certainly admire. So, instead of focusing on what you don't have, and instead of being jealous of other people and plotting for their fall, just channel all that energy into helping yourself be a better and stronger person. Focus on improving your skills instead of wishing for people to just be weak and disappear.

Believing in yourself is certainly one of the best things you can do in life.

Again, there are so many people in this world who are determined to bring you down—or who have nothing better to do than bash others and make these people feel bad about themselves. It sure is hard to be on the receiving end of this, but you have to realize that the only thing you can do for yourself is to actually stand up for who you are—and believe that you're worth it.

Here are some tips you could follow:

1.   Start letting go of your fears. Fears are pretty much your biggest limitations in life. Fears can stop you from doing what you want to do—and for making your dreams come to life.

Some people make use of fears as defence mechanism. For example, people who are afraid of rejection and failure just say that they're scared of something so they wouldn't have to do it. But, come to think of it, doing so would just lead you to bigger failures in the future because then, you are not going to do anything to change your life. This is why you need to learn how to move past the fears—and take action to reach your desired level of success! Try doing what's mentioned below:

Make a list of your fears.

Choose one of those fears that you can focus on at the moment, and then sit straight or lie down on your back. Close your eyes—but make sure that you wouldn't sleep.

Then, hold one part of your body (i.e., the toes, the knees), breathe deeply, and say: I welcome resistance and infuse it with love and light. Repeat until you feel relaxed.

Talk to the fear. Talk about why it's there, and why it became your fear in the first place. Thank it. Talk to the fear again. Say goodbye. Say you're ready to take charge of your life now. This way, you can finally heal and let go.

2.   Make way for some good self-talk! You know what's a common problem with most people? They fail to realize that they are not alone.

As a person, you're probably programmed to think that life is not good without friends, or without the company of other people, when in fact, the first relationship you have to nurture is the one you have with yourself.

Try to observe yourself for a couple of seconds and you'll notice that it's as if there's a monologue going on in your mind. This monologue goes on up until the time you go to bed, and that's why they say that you only have to think happy thoughts before going to bed so that those thoughts would be the first one's you'd invoke when you wake up the following morning.

For five minutes, do nothing but observe what's going on in your head. It does sound crazy, but hey, those 5 minutes could do a lot for your psyche! After minutes of observation, write down what you have been thinking or telling yourself. Write even about the bad things, and next to them, write about what you can tell yourself—instead of focusing on the negative stuff. Write about limitations. Read them. Once you do, you'll surely realize how limiting they are—and in that moment, you'd see that you actually want to do more than what you're limiting yourself to!

3.   Be more in control of your mind. One of the worst things you could make yourself believe is that you do not have control over your own mind. This is wrong.

You own your mind, and it does not own you. That in itself should make you realize that sometimes, the thoughts that you feed your mind are basically what drags it down. Remember that according to science, your brain is divided into two main parts, which are the conscious and the sub-conscious. Your conscious mind is only the one that sets goals, and actually just occupies 12% of the mind. It is what acts in the here and now, and does not have any long-term memory.

However, your subconscious mind is actually more important. Aside from occupying 88% of the mind, it is responsible for getting the job done. It handles all brain functions from the inside, and is an ultimate goal-getter. It never forgets. It holds all your memories, and makes you nostalgic. But you know what the great thing about it is? It is actually programmable—and that's why you have to take control of it, and feed it the right thoughts!

4.   Learn your leverage. Leverage basically means a series of steps you can take to change yourself—and how or why you are doing the said things. A person's reason for leverage can both come from pain and pleasure. Now, those two can be put together to create a mindset for success! For this, you could try asking yourself the following questions:

Write down your core beliefs in life. What motivates you towards pleasure and pain? (For example, if you know your job is hard, and yet you still do it—why? What does it give you? How does it make you feel?

Ask pain associating questions, such as:

What has this thing that you want cost you in the past?

What will it cost you now?

What is it costing you in? (family, friends, vehicles, items, etc.)

What is it costing the people that you love?

Ask pleasure-associating questions:

What will you gain from this thing that you like?

If you change this now, what would it do for your life?

What will this thing give you?

How does this thing make you feel?

What will this mean for the people around you?

Questions that denote inconsistency:

As a leader, how do you think your followers see you, knowing that you can have problems with self-discipline, too?

How does drinking keep you from being close with the ones you love?

How can drinking make you feel good when it makes the people around you uncomfortable?

As you may have noticed, these questions have a lot to do with psychology. By challenging yourself and with a little introspection, you're able to know what you're really committed to. By knowing what you're committed to, you can form new habits—habits that will definitely take you to success—and will help you stay positive even when times get hard!

5.	Make sure your goals are aligned with your mission and vision in life. One of the reasons why people get easily disappointed is that they cannot seem to achieve their goals because their goals are not in line with their mission and vision statement. Take note that every life has a purpose—and everything you do should coincide with the said purpose. This way, it would be easy for you to do whatever you can to attain those goals!

6.	Learn how to deal with failure. You know, getting comfortable with failures doesn't mean you are just going to allow yourself to fail. On the contrary, it means that even though you'd fail at times, you won't let those failures taint the way you think of yourself. Why? Because sometimes, no matter how hard you try, you'd still fail— but it does not mean that you're a failure. The outcomes are never really in your control, but how you turn yourself around, and make something out of even the worst things would define you as a person!

7.	Learn that success is different for everyone. Finally, in order to believe in yourself, you have to realize that your story is not the same as someone else's story. Even if someone has all the riches in the world, and you don't, it does not mean that you can't be considered successful yourself. What you have to realize is that every person in the world could be successful in their own right—in their own ways. You don't have to rush your success. No matter how many mishaps and failures you've had in your life, there's always time to make things better. You can always make things happen—just make sure to believe in yourself!

Believe in yourself and a lot of positive things would happen in your life—for sure!

One thing about people is that oftentimes, they become overly idealistic that they forget to ground themselves to the reality of life. If you are guilty of this, you probably should realize how damaging it could be.

You see, thinking positively is not about telling yourself to believe in things that are not true, but it's also not about trying to pick your life apart in any way you could. There really are things in life that you have no control over—and while that may be scary, it also reminds you that that's just the way life goes.

You can help yourself by not worrying too much—and just trying to expect the best in life, while working for it, of course.

Question Yourself

Try to ask yourself the following questions below so you could have a gist of what you are really like—and what life is like, as well. And when you get to understand what you can and cannot do, the chances of you being so worked up over things you have no control of will be lessened, too!

Which tasks do you avoid because you're not confident enough to do them?

Which personal resources do you have access to?

What new technology you know can help you? Do you have access to it?

What is one thing that you do that you know you do better than anyone else?

What do people often see as your weaknesses?

What do most people see as your strengths?

What connections do you have?

What are your negative work habits?

What are the challenges that you're currently facing at work?

What are the advantages in life that you know you have?

What are personality traits that you know hold you back?

Is your job/niche constantly changing?

Is there a kind of work that you want to do?

How do you think you're able to influence people?

How do you feel about the niche or industry that you're in? Do you think that it is growing? And, is it actually helping you grow?

Have you ever encountered the same complaints over and over again?

Does the constantly changing world make you feel threatened?

Could any of your weaknesses become detrimental in your life?

How to start expecting the best—while being prepared for the worst

A great attitude to have in life is to learn how to be prepared for the worst—but also know how to expect the best in life. Again, when you know who you are and what you can do, you won't put yourself in uncompromising situations—and you'd actually learn how to deal with the things in your life in the right way!

Try to review what you have done before. What were the mistakes you made in the past that you no longer want to repeat? How can you manage not to repeat them? By thinking back on what you've done, you'll get some clarity about what you're supposed to do.

Try to look at your life from afar. Ask yourself how you feel, and what makes you feel bad. Then, try to see if you could weed out some toxic people or situations in life.

Think outside the box. Maybe, you're not getting the results you want because you're thinking the same way as others. You don't have to do that. Remember that you can always create your own path and make your own ways.

Think about what you really want to do in life. Sometimes, you only get disappointed because of goals that you have not made come true yet. Break your goals down into smaller ones, and see what you can do each day that would benefit you in the long run.

Sometimes, expectations cause hurt. Make a list of your expectations, read them again, and check if they are actually doable or if they're too much. Remind yourself that everyone is a human—you cannot expect something that you yourself are not willing to give.

Remember that you are disappointed because you have feelings. That's okay. While things may not have gone your way today, just think about the fact that they can be better tomorrow. Every day is different!

Put yourself in other people's shoes. It is such a cliché, but it works. Once you learn to put yourself in other people's shoes, you also begin to see how their mind works. When people around you make certain decisions that make you raise your eyebrows, understand where they are coming from. Remember they are not you.

Make an effort. Maybe, you're lonely because you feel alone and you aren't making progress in life. Well, make an effort to put yourself out there. Talk to people. Write your mission and vision in life. Get to know yourself better. Help someone in need.

Listen—and also learn how to open up.

If number 1 is not possible, get a piece of paper or a journal and write about how you feel. Exorcise your demons.

Communicate the hurt. You can either talk to the person who hurt you, or someone you trust. Let things out and air your side.

Be curious about the people you meet. Do not see them as plain strangers, but rather as people who are also going through things. Remember that each person you see has a story.

Be ambiguous. Learn to see different sides of any given situation. This doesn't mean you're going to side with the bad people, but rather that you'd also learn to see what made them that way—or why things ended up this way.

Remember that you are enough. Don't push yourself too hard, but don't slack off, either. Just do what you can!

Chapter 9 Express Gratitude

And finally, learn how to be grateful!

A person who's full of gratitude is someone who knows how to appreciate what he has. Being content does not mean you're not going to do anything to change your life, but is actually a way of letting joy into your life.

According to the Chinese Philosopher Lao Tzu, a person becomes truly rich when he realizes that he actually has enough. This means that each day of your life, it's best that you cultivate the attitude of gratitude!

To do so, you can follow the guidelines below:

1. String a couple of beads, and think about who and what you're thankful for as you run your fingers on each of the beads.

2. Moments are fleeting. They'll pass by—and sooner or later, you'd regret the fact that you chose to be sad when really, you could've just been happy! As cliché as it sounds, laughter really is the best medicine. It's so important to allot a few minutes, and even seconds of your day to laughter. Look for funny videos online, talk to people and have animated conversations, and just realize that in order for you to be happy, you have to learn how to stop worrying about every single thing and learn how to laugh at your problems, not because you're trying to escape from them, but because you know that sooner or later, you'll be able to fix them and move on with your life.

3. Don't thrive on drama! Don't thrive on drama and don't think that just because something feels like it's in the movies does it mean

that you have to feel like it's okay to be stuck in those situations for life. Don't let your situation in life define who you are, and don't let those situations limit you with what you can do.

4. Realize that not everyone has what you have. Stop looking for what you don't have and start appreciating what you have right now.

5. Create your gratitude wheel. Think of a colour wheel, but instead of colours, categorize the wheel depending on who and what you're thankful for in your life!

6. Remember that little things are also big things. Sure, you're not a millionaire yet, but you have enough money to drive you by. Or, what about the fact that the person you like smiled at you, or your boss told you that he believes in you? Those little things are enough to be thankful for—and are enough to make you happy. It's not settling—it's appreciating.

7. Keep a gratitude journal. Write down anything you're thankful for— and make sure to do it each day.

8. You can choose to be happy. You can choose to focus on the good stuff, instead of wallowing in things you cannot fix right away.

9. Keep a Gratitude Rock. It could be a piece of marble, a small clean rock—anything that you can keep in your pocket or your purse. The key here is to remember to be thankful for even the smallest things in life—every time you touch the rock! For example, the fact that you woke up this morning, how you got to work early, some spare change—anything!

See? There are so many things that you can do each day to help yourself be grateful! A grateful person is a master of his emotions—and that's certainly what you'd like to be!

Be thankful for each day of your life and for what you have. This way, you would see that life was created for your glory—and you'd realize what a valuable thing it is to actually be alive and have the chance to savour life for what it is!

Conclusion

Thank you again for downloading this book!

I hope this book was able to help you to understand how positive thinking can help you make your life better.

The next step is to make sure that you keep the tips mentioned here in mind—so you could give yourself the chance to live the life that's meant for you—and the life that you really want!

Finally, if you enjoyed this book, then I'd like to ask you for a favour, would you be kind enough to leave a review for this book on Amazon? It'd be greatly appreciated!

Click here to leave a review for this book on Amazon!

Thank you and good luck!

Check Out My Other Books by Dylan j Cameron

SELF-DISCIPLINE, Get Control of Yourself by Dylan j Cameron

Alpha Male. How to become more confident and live the life you deserve. By Dylan j Cameron

Made in the USA
Middletown, DE
06 December 2017